THE VINE COMEDY

A DISCORD DANCE

A. M. K. ABERDEEN

The Vine Comedy

A Discord Dance

A. M. K. Aberdeen

Table of Contents

Dedication   V
"Somewhere between you & I"   V

Part One   1
"Somewhere between Heaven and Hell"   1

Part Two   51
"Somewhere between Earth and Hell"   51

Part Three   97
"Somewhere between History and Humility"   97

™ DIADEM MEDIA LLC., ©2018

This edition published in 2018 by

™ Diadem Media limited ®, LLC,.

3 – 1501 Dupont Avenue Toronto Ontario m6p 3s2

Copyright © Diadem Media Limited / Aisha M. Aberdeen

All rights reserved, no part of this publication may be reproduced, stored in a retrieval system, or transmitted, in any form or by any means, electronic, mechanical, photocopying, recording or otherwise, without written permission in accordance with the provisions of the Copyright Act of 1965 (as amended). Any person or persons who do any unauthorized act in relation to this publication may be liable to criminal prosecution and civil claims for damages.

Typesetting by: Diadem Media [Publishers]

Cover image: A. M. K. Aberdeen

Isbn: 978-7753325-0-3

Dedication

"Somewhere between You & I"

The Vine Comedy, A Discord Dance is dedicated to my daughter - K. A. You are my greatest inspiration. Love, Mom

&

To my father, thank you for the blessing of rhythm and rhyme. Love, Your Daughter

&

To The Almighty, Thank you, for Life. Love, Daughter of Your Light.

The Vine Comedy

A Discord Dance

Part One

"Somewhere between Heaven and Hell"

Ibliss argued with God,

"Humans' aren't worth it,

You'll give them Light

And they'll sell their

Souls' for trinkets"!

You'll give them warmth

And they'll share

Diseased, blankets.

They all wont say psalms,

They're not all like David.

Da wood – The Void,

They'll choose darkness.

Mankind is haphazard

and heartless.

Let me display, add to their test.

God you made Tin Men,

With no hearts in their chest,

All brass I bet, Mule headednessss".

And God, smiled sunlight
Answered Ibliss.

"Tin Men cause

SIN came in them,

You'll understand this.

My word and kindness,

I placed in their breast.

Even if you took their minds,

For their whole life,

They'll remember me in death.

I called them Man Kind in Genesis.

For many are added,

Like Mani and Moses,

And to women, I gave grace

More beautiful than Roses,

An within their hearts,

They'll always know where home is"

God smiled sunlight,

Looked upon Ibliss.

"Ibliss you'd have to sell bliss,

Wrench out their hearts,

Make them aimless.

But I God promise them a new heart,

A mansion in my kingdom of greatness,

No man's son will lead

Them to Zion,

All mind stateless,

All man kind mine.

You're arguments baseless,

And in time you too,

Will see the faceless,

Am, God the Nameless,

Clouds dust at my feet,

Do you know what the rainbow is?

Humanity may go low,

Create a rainbow endless.

All colors create light.

Am, God the nameless.

In a grain of sand,

The universe is magnified.

There's no faithless,

Man's works speak,

He can remain soundless.

Man's anger peaks,

My love is boundless,

For them I separated

The light, from the darkness.

No radiant stones

I removed your garments,

No place to call home

No ancient Eden,

Oh Ibliss how far you've fallen.

Always in Babel,

No fruit of wisdom.

You rule the dirt,

And produced not a,

Mud brick kingdom.

I God made man from mud,

Mix it with wisdom".

God said proudly,

Smile unhidden.

"Now look, how many

Man he made,

And you still can't see,

My heart's in them.

You won't declare my art is them!

Then and always will be

A perfect, representation of me".

God shook his head,

Pursed his lips

"Without eyes Ibliss

What do you see?

Without your raiment

Can you understand me?

The earths a foot stool

And you're under my feet.

I made man from the dust of the earth

And that's your meat.

When you strike her ankles

She will stomp you with her feet.

I made the dust of the earth into man

Without me you couldn't eat.

Ibliss, does horses endear fleas?"

Ibliss anger rose between his teeth.

"Ss ss savior,

You also made me".

God smiled sun,

"Only to test them

But you still will not see,

Milk stirred is butter,

What settles is cheese.

I am the measure,

By which they are judge.

Ibliss who judges me?

You are a flame

Near a potters wheel.

Crucible's I pass them through fires,

They come out pristine.

Crucify my child,

You'll encourage them,

After I brought them

Through, a bloody sea.

None look upon my face,

None care for my tears to see.

I wept for Noah

And drowned the earth

Only I God is master of me.

You led some astray

    Iron mingled with clay,

An unholy potters wheel.

Sent vines amongst my groves,

To strangle, all my trees.

Stunt the branches,

An manipulate the seeds,

Ibliss this is your purpose

You have no hope,

In worshipping me.

Like a worm you'll churn the mud,

To aerate the seeds,

And they'll bury their roots,

Near my feet.

And when my light touches them,

Warmth hearts will push forth leaves.

And from the mud,

The strongest trees

Will rise to praise me

And from the mud

On worms and slugs

The birds will be left to feed

Some birds will swallow stones,

Forever looking for home

Chicken climbing trees,

Nesting among the

Branches of seeds

Their meant to eat".

G od questioned

"Ibliss, what is man to me?

I made him on the sixth day

I gave him two eye, two ears

Two nostrils to breathe

One mouth because he is free.

I set him on the sixth ball

And with one tongue he praises me

Ten fingers and ten toes

They dedicate their works to me

And when they vent in woe

My children cry to me

I reduce their oppressors

And they remember they are free

Some time they lose their way

But in them I placed a beacon

Everyone of them can see

Their light shines brighter,

Than any of your lost stones,

Would ever be.

You are a darkness they will never see"

God said in test,

"Excuse me Ibliss"

But Ibliss sucked his teeth

Ibliss lacked manners.

So God spoke quietly.

"Ibliss you are not man,

You have no manners

You still cannot wait patiently?

You can only be a charmer,

So I'll help you to read.

You spell your name,

C HARMER.

Forever more, eve will know,

You only mean to harm her.

She'll still strike your head,

Always a blow,

She'll teach some of her,

Children to charm yah,

And you think she follows,

What you do to her

She surely return the favor,

I told you

Hell hath no wrath

Like a woman scorned"

    God smiled and laughed,

"You're right to call me

Ss, ss, savior.

She'll bring you to ruin

I know because am her maker,

Differently and lastly I created her.

She'll trick a dragon to her tower,

Damsel in distress with power.

Anger will make you rake up a flower

But you lack manners

Must I go over?

Your inhumane nature,

Your rebellious character,

I made man, kind,

With a Godly character,

You'll be unhinged all the time.

You cannot make matter

Intricate, animate

Compassionate, kind

Man is kind

Cause I named him mine

And if am love

Man I must have place love in

And kind

Ibliss to mans' ways

You'll remain blind.

Am God,

And for me, you refused

To stay in line.

Now you're screaming screeches

No heavenly chimes.

Funny how you lost

You're voice,

When I gave man

Wind from mine.

Ibliss you have no choice,

But I God gave free will,

To man's lineage line.

I made him a minute,

Reflection of myself

The divine.

For man I parted,

The waters from the waters,

The void from light,

I saw that it was good,

An Adam declare me right.

Ibliss when asked

The same question

You answered me in spite

Anger in your breast

T' was me you wanted to fight

In pride you say

You'd mount up to this height

You'd dash my throne in pieces

My kingdom, your heist

You're the sinner

Man's right"

Ibliss bowed his head

He'd say in prayer

God knew it was fright

Adam and God knew his mind

Before he took flight

Again anger rose in Ibliss

Adam's sons' will have the sight

Adam saw Ibliss was naked

Lost his garment of light

God looked at Ibliss with kindness

"You'd have to walk in darkness and night

Be despised by widows, husbands and wives

Malfeasant miscreant

Blamed for miscarriages all your life

You mismanaged Eden

You'll pay a high price

You loaned out my vineyards

In Baal' Hamon now they sell rice

Little babes lost in mud puddles

Tormented like mice

Ibliss in your hands at night"

Ibliss shamefully looked away

God saw what he did that day

When he tormented a little girl

And mice

God laughed and smiled

"Ibliss that's the

Extent of your might

Your life will be sad

Where you go there'll be blithe

And when a person

Become's raving mad

I'd know it's with you they

Having a fight

For you I made raving mad

To put my throne in your sight!

Gave you a golden voice

And a holy Timbrel as lungs

Wind Pipes"

Ibliss fell before God

"Master singing was my life

the winds of my lungs were nothing like

Pity was seen if you

Could see the face of God

But none beholds' his sight

God shook his head, shone light

"Given you're so attached to the wind

A spirit of the wind tormentuous

Shall be your life

Hot winds in the air of earth

Be it left or right

Hot winds in man's ear

To create strife"

God knew Ibliss still sought

To justify wrong as right

So god brought the choir forth

"Ibliss if you can see

Find your spot

Amongst all their light"

Ibliss fell even more

God's grace no longer holding him upright

God's choir master maestro

Couldn't stand upright?

No Holy Ghost in windpipes

No longer a part of the Holy Host

Ibliss shook his coil

"God I've no Hype"

No beats no drums

No Timbrels no sounds

"God what have you done to my life?"

God patiently waited

Ibliss anger was unabated

"Master it is not my fault

I can't fall in line

You created me like this

Aren't I fruit.

Although,

Lemons and limes?

God kept it simple

"Broken vessels no

Longer hold wine

Salt of the earth mine

Dust be the meal of thine"

Ibliss moved, but God knew

What was in his mind.

"Must you try to kneel Ibliss?

You no longer have a spine"

"Ss ss ss" he tried to sing

But his words were serpentine

And for all he knew he couldn't think

Not but the unkind

In his belly bile brew

And God spoke as he knew

"Bitter will be his vine

Haters of mankind,

Forever seeking a sign,

To the end of the world

They'll try to corrupt my time,

Shortens man life,

Gave Man a vain lie line,

If Ibliss only knew

He'd willingly become blind

"You'd come to watch your

Creations destroyed in time.

There's a lesson

Never you question

The divine

Am, the Almighty

I make the rules

And I choose to be

Merciful and kind

All you've ever seen

I made from my mind

I made you from smokeless fire

The winds from the sublime

I made ether

Everywhere and still in line

I fashioned the universes

And every verse sung before its' time

I made what you cannot fathom

A Discord Dance

And a fathom you've become

I made the waters, call her Nun

And when Moses crossed over her

With many daughters' and sons'

I gave her permission, as orders

Have your waters,

Reverse their run.

And when they crossed over

We didn't lose one,

Not one drop wasted

I fashioned Nun

I put a leash on leviathan

When the world was over run.

Ibliss you still lack reason

And wisdom is not your companion

I made you just for a season

I'd always be man's champion.

You could lead them astray

I'll deliver each and every one

I told you Eve outwitted you,

Took hold of your

Princely garments

A naked king – without clothes

Disrobe a fallen one

Crush your head

Bruised your ego

Rejected by woman.

The first Mada,

Loves Adam

The two become one

And in Able all their

Works' was near done

You're hate will

Forever go after

The Abel'd

Label The holy

The crazy one

But my love for his parents

Held my hand

I didn't smite

A first-born son

Ibliss when will you learn

It's by my mercy

The universe is hung

And whose, close to me

To comprehend my wisdom?

If the world but a foot-stool

The heavens but a throne

Can you comprehend,

The breath and length

Of my kingdom?

Look how arrogant you get

When you're just a speck

Of my wisdom?

Ibliss you'd have to live many lives

To be just and wise

To even see the

Castle's in my Mansion"

Ibliss cried,

Weeping

"Master you lie"!

God voice rose

More than the heavenly

Choir composed

He spoke truth and vision

"Ibliss just so you know

I speak clearly you'd

Never suppose

But in mansion

Is Man and Zion,

My kingdom".

Ibliss then came to know

Only a glint of the glow

He screamed out in woe

Instantly, he was silenced.

Small snake mind

Too much to hold

G od smiled,

"Ibliss you are the only creature

I made prideful and bold.

Thus you'll be led by the fold,

You are the darkness

I separated, from,

The light of old

Before I God fashioned the world

I saw and I know

That separation was good

You're argument with me

About man's manhood

Is baseless and its obvious

My creation to you

Is not understood

For many lives you'd

Roam the waste".

Ibliss

Breathe sharp

Emerged from his chest

"Yes"

Ibliss lost his argument

"Many lives" he croaked

"then, yes"

God smiled sunlight

At the choir

"Messengers of God the nameless"

Ibliss no longer heard God's voice

Amongst their merriness

God smiled "tell Ibliss

To measure my kingdom

If he could find it."

Laughing he threw

An Almond stick

"And tell him to use this".

With Almond stick

And message in his breast

Ibliss set about

To complete his test

He walked the length,

And the breath

And still could not manifest

A single number,

Not even an estimate.

Ibliss lost his sense,

He was

Holy breath Less

Numb and cold.

Coiled the heartless

He was more

Angered

Than before

Screaming breathless

Seething in his chest

Irony

He had a rod

He couldn't measure with.

Ibliss screamed to God

"I'd rather measure with a sword"

I'd put your children

Throats to it!

The clouds closed above

From the thrushes flew a dove

And Ibliss knew his

Words' was witnessed.

Rain fell to the earth

Blessing mans hurt

Cursing Ibliss worth.

His only option

The rock or the dirt.

Ibliss piqued up

"I'd be a rock.

Jagged un cut

I'd await the saviors' birth

I'd fashion a knot a noose,

He's loose

No hiccups

I'll be there first

For the cross,

The lumber I'll cut

"What's man worth?

God's' first question popped up

Ibliss laughed

"Pieces of silver

Not even an ingot"!

His laughter was sinister

"I'll drive them crazy

Have them reading inkblots

Tea-leaves and tea pots

God think I could

Measure with this Rod?

I Ibliss thinks' not"

He threw the rod behind him

He didn't look back to the spot

The dove cooed in peace

And from the Rod a leaf popped up

Light shone from heaven

Illuminating the spot.

Ibliss knew something change

But he couldn't really stop

His mind was craze

In a daze

A new plan he develop

'I'll cut down every tree

The savior of man

Would not get a cot

And for rest

He will not get

He won't be able to flee

Any spot"

The rain fell harder

Ibliss muddy enough

Screamed to the heavens

"An every stream and river

I'll dry shut up

Your children will walk the deserts

An water they'll have to buy a cup"

Ibliss laughed as it rained

Evil words he knew a lot

"I'll bring your children in chains

To Sodom

And you'll have to burn them up"

Ibliss laughed

Even more brave, or was it craze

God know

A lightening hit the spot

Ibliss coiled and he hiss

Frightful fear

Boiled within his stomach

The lightening hisses louder

"You will not insult The Creator

Another word and I'll fry you up"

God laughter held the shower

Light, lightening and power

In essence God stopped her

"Of his mess, worry not,

For all the seas and the trees,

My son's will clean it up,

And in time Ibliss will be weary

He kicks rocks because he can't hear me

Look closely

He's walking in my clock,

Worst yet

He's on the same spot

And the Almond stick

Has already grew up

Put forth fruit, which riseth up

Spreadeth its branches

An in growing, it has not stopped

    God laughed, Ibliss has no roots

How can he grow up?

God smiled sunlight

And the Almond tree

Dropped another fruit

Near the spot

Ibliss felt the vibration

In his scales

And in fear he looked up

An around, his eyes saw the spot

He sought shelter

Under its shade

The fruit fell on his head

Crushed

Ibliss slithered away.

Bruised and confused

God laughed

"Prophecy will never stop"

The clouds parted

The sunrays praised

Ibliss knew

Another of God's laws, was laid

His chest, he tried to puff up

But falling to the floor

Slipped, he bit the dust

Falling down a cliff

Two many light years

He seemed to drop

Slithering and sliding

No fingers to cling

No feet to stand up

Crashed in a daze

Hung and clung to the

First thing his serpentine

Coils touched

The Tree tried

To shake him off

Stubborn mule refused to drop

Coiled to the branches

Ibliss chose his spot

The tree called to the creator

"Tell him to get off"

"It'll be my pleasure,

But I sent him to measure

He searching out my wisdom

Am certain he'll soon

Ask you for paper

In Ibliss bitter

Heart he thought

He knew

Certain t' was a clue

The tree, he began to shake her

"God to what cost

This buffoons' at a lost

He's an old hater

Seeking wisdom and paper"

The tree spoke, and I

Only have figs and dates

Ibliss hearing the tree speaking

And no one was he seeing

Anger seething

He figured "I'd wait here"

For the first time

T' was though he was thinking

Ibliss hissed

"I know God is somewhere near"

S o when prayerful singing

Filled his ear

He was convinced

"The holy choir is here"

The singing got nearer

It brought him some cheer

He shook the tree's branches

Without much a care

What came to his sight,

He couldn't compare

The female Adam drew

Ever so near

Ibliss snarled breath

"T' was her who stole my flare"

And with an evil eye

Ibliss did glare

Eve sung sweetly

Him she didn't hear

Ibliss was irate

He rattled and snare

The tree called

To God Almighty

"Ibliss is acting all weird"

God gave a nod and a sun filled glare

Eve radiated

Her beauty was bare

Ibliss rattled even more

"I'll have to set a snare"

Adam's half walked

And sung with the

Birds of the air

She didn't think once

Danger was near

Walking and singing

Her innocence was rare

Coming to The Tree

She marveled without fear

"What is your name?

Adam

Named all that is here"

Ibliss wasn't tamed

And he showed his anger

"What's in a name?"

Eve erupted into laughter

"Adam named everything made

By The Creator

What has no name does not matter"

Eve spoke physics

But Ibliss heard laughter

"Well if, if a names' important

Then um, am the great measurer"

Eve laughed further

"Why do you need to measure?"

Just ask The Creator"

Eve laughed to her fill

Sitting for leisure

Ibliss heart blazed

"I'll, I'll, have my measure"

He said to himself

Almost a whisper

Eve laughed 'he didn't understand'

Ibliss the only sinner

Eve laughter died down

By then Ibliss was beyond sinister

"God has a test

He sent me to administer

You did well

Only the rod's the measurer"

Eve looked at him odd

'Eh Either way you're the winner"

Ibliss stuttered to cover

"Here have some fruit,

Adam will have some later"

Ibliss spoke fast

"You came first

Adam's asleep in the pasture"

Eve was perplexed

No longer in laughter

"What is this test?

Why is Adam asleep in the pasture"?

Ibliss was ignorant he had no answer

Truth be told, he was going off anger

Now he tried, but he already lied earlier

And eve was soon to realized

For even his name he had no answer

He stammered a word

"Wisdom"

A fruit in his coil's like charmer.

Eve spoke softly

"God gives wisdom"

Ibliss spoke quickly

"And I, was once his messenger"

Eve thought it odd,

Ibliss said once

She repeated, "once a messenger"

Ibliss stammered quietly

"She'll figure me out"

Then he shouted

"But now am greater"

Eve muttered "how come?"

Truly Ibliss had no answer

He repeated what he recalled

"A test, a Rod,

A fruit did fall"

He said with a nod

"You see and now am greater"

Truth be told

Ibliss was an old hater

Eve wore a radiant glow

That reminded Ibliss of home

And now he wanted to disrobe her

"Eat and you'll know the answer"

Ibliss said with glee

Eve bit and fell to her knees

Her garment of youth

Torn un-seemingly

Ibliss slithered down the tree

"You, ss, ss, see, I freed ya"

Eve bit and saw

What the heavens abhor

Seeing Ibliss worse than before

A curse amongst

The heavenly choir

What's worst he envied God

And in Adams work he's

Been finding fault

He was forever shut out of

The heavenly sky vault

And Eve heart hung heavy

She'll be forever at fault

The tree shook Ibliss of off

Just because

The sun beamed bright

On Adam by the water

"Adam this is almighty god"

Adam looked up, answered

With a nod

"Yes father my God?"

God smiled sunlight

"Adam Eve may need your comfort

Ibliss lost his rod

And he's making her upset"

Adam spoke, "he's such a kid

Doesn't know water is wet

Thinks for every thing he

Has to take a step

Father your tears will fill the earth

And he'll still be hateful I bet,

For your tears, man knows' no plug

Ibliss know not water is wet"

Adam spoke as he walked

"God I will prevent Eve

From staying upset"

He was certain Ibliss would leave

With every stride and step

When Adam arrived,

Eve was having a fit

Fruits were flying here and there

Adam stammered from his lips

"Eve pelts, and kicks"?

The closer he got,

The more he could see

Eve was stomping on Ibliss

The tree was shaking off her fruits

Laughing in a fit

Through her laughter

The tree was complaining

"An he shook me miss,

He lied on the Almighty

God The Nameless

You're right to give him licks"

Eve struck Ibliss

Head with a fruit

And was about to give him a kick

Adam held her hand

He made a demand

"Ibliss what's all of this?"

Ibliss was stunned

His serpentine tongue

Was not thankful to the man

"Ss ss SALAM ADAM"

God made his mouth command

For in truth, Ibliss was prepared

To accused Eve

The words he sought to say

Was "me she slammed"

Truly it was god who held eve's hand

For Ibliss would have gone beyond dust

He would have been turned to sand

Eve was not intending to leave Ibliss

To bring her children harm

God shone sunlight on everything

But couldn't bring Ibliss warmth.

God knew what he'd do for his children,

Ibliss knew not the extent of Gods' wisdom.

He coiled in shame, somewhat shocked by the sun

He rose and flail, as though charmed stunned

Eve sucked in her breath, and leaning to Adam

"Name him Satan, ... Hun

NAHASH, Ibliss, NATAS

My children will know everyone"

Ibliss was angry,

"That, woman had nerve

He slithered off,

I'll remember her words

Each name I'll make a curse"

His belly scratching against the dirt

Within his veins he felt hurt

But instead of weeping he only cursed

Seeking out stones of his former worth

He dug himself deeper into the dirt

He fell as he scrambled,

Slithered and curse

Each stone he found he threw up onto the earth

None shone like his former garment

"Where did Eve get hers?"

Ibliss slithered across the expanse of the earth

He searched

"How could this be I must still have worth?

Where god placed me I must measure my worst?"

Ibliss shame even his head hurt

"Measure what god made better?

Am lost with out hope"

He sunk deeper, covered in scales

"I can't measure weight or worth"

So fumbling he wanted to erase

Ego and hurt

"Am, my own savior,

I'll make my own shirt"

He scratched with his tail

And head in the dirt

Only dust flew

Ibliss knew

He was lost and cursed

He muttered to himself

Striking a stone

T he stone screamed out to God in wailing woe

"He lost his garments now its me he provokes?"

Laughing God quietly spoke

"Humble stone, may I tell you a joke?"

God whispered "Ibliss already

Answered my riddle

But he's too filled with anger

And I made him simple"

The stone smiled

"God you gave me a dimple,

Is someone going to tell him"

The stone tried, and God smile

"you see

He's too simple

He'd have to watch his words

Live out his curse

Calm down as he walk

Tthe circle of the earth

Ibliss ego is only what's hurt

And his mind and mouth makes it worse

He's ignorant so expect his rants to get worst

Until then, just think him cursed"

Ibliss walked and hissed his hurt

He wandered until he came upon

Eve singing happily, playing with her sons

Eve heart was filled with a love so pure

None can over come

Yet Ibliss saw her merriness

And gave chase to one of her sons

Trapped, Cain screamed out

For the help of his mom

His call was too late

Ibliss bit made his ankle numb

Eve looked over her shoulders

"Where is the other one?"

As she spoke Cain awoke

Stuttering, "here, here I am mom"

Eve thought it odd

Her son's had no stammer

When they spoke.

Later she'll complain to Adam

"Cain feels numb and cold,

His temperature decreased

And his radiant glow"

If either had a dream

They'll make the other know

As the years went on, colder

Did Cain grow

So many times in his dreams

A snake came selling bliss and hope

Cain dream't a dream

That he couldn't let them know

Then one day,

Too soon it seemed

Able no longer play

In the field

A Sheppard and sheep

Life was good,

He had no groans

He came that day

Upon his brother Cain

Burying a stone

"Is that what,

You plan to offer

To God the Father?"

Able held a questioning look

Cain screamed out, "it's mine!

It'll grow in time

My dreams teach me

The riddle, The rhyme"

To Able Cain had lost his mind

He led sheep, though none were blind

A Discord Dance

What could Cain eat of a stones kind?

Able knew Cain wouldn't reap

Even if stones chimed

So patiently

Able turned aside

"Almighty God, explain to me why

My brother plants stones and glitters his eyes?"

God answered Able, not too concerned, with a smile

"Cain that one, Ibliss made numb, as a child"

God looked at Cain,

"Son soon, you'll go wild

Where's your brother?

Cain hissed, Jagged rock in his fist

Blood curled lips

"Am no keeper, An Able no brother of mine"

He was so numb,

God declared him vagabond

Because to Ibliss, he was tied.

The earth shook and God cried

A sacred tomb, he placed Able inside.

Though Seth was born,

Their pain was never to hide

Cain took Able, their love

And Ibliss took Cain, their pride

T' was a cave,

That Eve did morn inside.

For all the children she did bore,

The pain she never could hide

From that moment on

When ever she walked

Adam was at her side.

And as much as he walked

He talked to make her smile

"Do you remember?

Ibliss thought you tender

Before his head you did strike?

Ibliss lost every jewel,

He doesn't have a stripe

Look God replaced Able

He'll make things in time be all right"

Eve spoke sadly

"He'll go after our children

Even in the night"

Adam looked at Eve

"God made us in the Light"

He gave her hand a squeeze

"He'll make them be upright

Sure Ibliss will test them

Such was written in the prophecy past"

Adam looked at Eve with love

"Eve T' was you God made last

Before he rested and laughed

Before Ibliss got tested and path

Eve you, God made last
Like a builder builds a house
Am, a cornerstone and you're my half
And still the half God made last
Took you from under my heart
Ibliss call's me Tin Man
I call you God's Art"

      And then the clouds part

God smiled sunlight filled the world

They even heard God laugh.

Part Two

"Somewhere between Earth and Hell"

And as Adams sons' grew,

And Eve daughters' too.

Ibliss walked over the earth

Passing through and through.

All the works of man,

God bless in truth,

An all the children of Eve,

Knew Satan from their youth.

As they toiled the earth

Ibliss anger grew.

Hiss coiled of no worth

A belly of bitter brew

And watching Eve's children

He knew what he had to do.

One by one, They,

He started to persecute.

He stood on God Altar

Strange fire of Abihu

As Haman he tempted Ahasuerus

Esther had to marry a king

To protect her kindred

The Jews.

Separate light from darker

God said put a marker to Ahihud.

And on the covenant

He said put a seal to

Nehemiah and Beninu.

Ibliss seethe he had no root.

He was the darkeneth counsel

Of Job's friend Elihu

He spoke of revolt

In the tongue of Gashmu.

God Favor shown in Caleb

And his first born son Iru.

But Ibliss insist

The foreign-tongued

Wife of Jaasu

God decreed

Good indeed the

Turning back of Jashub,

Hateful Ibliss with no law of God

Walked in Jehu,

And who really knew

If as Malluch

He walked in Melicu,

Ibliss hissed, anger

His 'offspring's were seen by Raphu'

Midnight Mid life Phineas slew

Midianite and Zimri Son of Salu

From Noah to Lot

He still hadn't got a clue.

God light shone

He already knew

David will be praised

Near and Far,

Even by King Tou.

Returned from Zerubbabel

And captivity the family of Zatthu

Redemption to the chosen few

Repentance Ibliss never knew.

Ibliss couldn't bless,

Just bliss he sold to those

Who sought the Truth,

And all Eve's daughters'

He pursued and persecute

Making widows of Naomi,

Orpah and Ruth,

She could not return to Moab.

Tied God's law an mother-in-law

Was Ruth

Yet Ibliss hate hissed, insist

He sought wisdom

On hills tempted Solomon

But only Sheba gained

The proof

The more he sought,

The more he found

The Almighty's reproof

Wisdom and God's grace,

Boundless!

God's love had no Roof.

From the darkness and

Through the years,

Arrows,

Ibliss learnt to Shoot.

Tempted pharaohs,

And kings

Saul had David pursued.

As midwife's stifled

The life

Of, wee little Hebrews

As mother and wife of

Ungodly Jehoiakim

Nehushta, Satan,

The brass Nahash,

Showed a sharp tooth.

Without need for

Further proof

God breathe into

The Almond shoot

"I God sent you all as prophets

"Prophesy the destruction

of all of it!

From mountains

To cities,

To seas

With listless ships,

Not One, Escapes it!

I'd grant you years

Amongst the vipers pit

See their ways, take none of it.

Talk when I say speak

Say anything else

And I'll close your lips.

They'll use and abuse you

And you'll take their hits.

Subtle I made your heart

They'll have none of it.

I sent them Christ

They found a whip

Remember child I hardened

Their hearts

And made them sick.

Made them full with empty

Rhetoric's, Gimmicks

Tell them the God that created

The heavens and the earth

Broken sticks and even dirt

Has weighed and measured

And found their worth

Haters of life

With wrath they fill

The earth

So my wrath will

Take them first.

Have they not found cities,

Under the dirt?

Measured my earth?

Cities, under seas?

I made blackness

And water first

Created many colors

In lights birth

Each being born under

A spectrum of light burst

Spectrums gives' all which

Is on this earth

Green foliage

Photosynthesize worth

Infrared, I made

Into a rose

Do they know what blue,

And purple light is worth?

Who knows' what type of life

Gamma rays' birth?

Can Ibliss kind be wrapped,

In my shirt?

Hide in my skirts?

Magnify my worth

Or imagine my hurt?

Bind leviathan

Or unbound a curse?

Has Ibliss kind stood

In the Center of the earth?

No!

Ibliss kind has divided my herd

Dishonored my word

Kill more of my sheep

Than I preferred

Fell into darkness

Found the void good

Only tyranny understood?

They harkened, not unto gladness

Pour cups of badness

A boy for wine and a girl sold?

They think me unaware

Grand-parent gone slow?

I am Ancient of Days of Old

I'd repay all of their ways

Let them know.

They'll shake and crumbled

When I glow

Darkness flees from light,

You know?

Who live outside my grace,

Do show?

Who can look upon my face,

Do you know?

Where is the place you can,

Hide and go?

What have you made,

On the earth from nothing

Do show?

Forethought the earth

And, the day of your birth?

Fore bare the many years of hurt?

To the garden I made Eden

And called the earth?

Prepare Gaia and you destroy

Make her of baseless worth

    Filled crystal streams with

 Muddy deeds?

Bloodies my seas?

For, black pearls?

Destroyed the dreams

Of young girls?

My wrath too soon unfurl

Upon the evil of this world

They disgrace my name

Said their evil

Was God ordained.

Predetermined in my name?

Preacher, predator, poacher

Wolves kept the sheep tamed?

Sheppard's' fled, they feared

More, than my name?

Gnawed at the marrow

The Judges did the same?

Innocence you made into a game?

How you treat the least of them

You treated me

My Prophets,

Tell them this

I gave into Solomon's hands

Of all Djinns even unto Ibliss

I commanded Queen Sheba

to test him, With her lips

Wise men lose kingdoms

By women's wits

And I God blessed it

Samson told Delilah

His most precious secret

Jonah obey by the belly

Of a fish

Joshua men stayed alive

Through a harlots lips

Israel lot grew a lot

    Code of the window

Wall and cord of scarlet

Always remember who'd

You call harlot

Tamar made certain Judah's

Line were not forgot

And a maid in the desert

Deserted held Ishmael's cot

Abandoned and alone

They were left to not

Yet I god gave

Them sup

Heir children like

The stars of heaven

Who can count the lot?

I sent Melchizedek to Abram

He gave me all the spoils he got

I promised unto him

Your lineage be the foundation rock.

And I delivered for him

Backsliding lot.

When Sodom and Gomorrah fell

He did not.

I found the needle in the hay

Before I sent

Brimstone and fire to the lot

I always repay

Innocence will not be left

to maggots

To rot.

Children I planted like flowers

Loudly they sing

"Father forget me not"

I gave every grass an angel

The bees did not forgot

They tend every flower with pollen

While Ibliss kind's pulls them up?

Every order I gave a color

Ibliss kind mixed them up

Every daughter I gave

To her mother

Ibliss kind plucks them up

Every season set in order

I God establish Cronos clock.

On this globe I set

The temperature.

To upright Job I God

Sent the tempter.

To Solomon I did

Send Holy Sophia.

Wrapped up in his ego

As Queen of Sheba.

Manifested into ether

How did he greet her?

These are the times if you see her

An evil generation looks

For a sign,

Imprinted into matter

Couldn't care for my words"

Verse and chorus

Hearse with chapter

Hoarse and hurt

The Prophets stammered

Their words

"God Man Matters!

Ibliss made some loathe"

Twas Enoch who first spoke

"Adonai I don't deny

Children of Giants

In gore and blood

Drenched the earth.

An of course

Separated iron ore

Taught blood mixed roots and curse

Cain has forgotten the law

And his off-springs sings

With bliss, Ibliss forbidden verse"

God's wisdom led with words

"Bid Them Curse!

And of you prophets

Some will have to live.

Through the worst

Hosea you go unto

The harlot the night nurse

My child your savior

Will be sold for silver

Judas the right purse.

And unto you Isaiah

They dilute the wine

With water,

The silver,

Dross Unrefined.

Rulers who chase after

Gifts and bribes

Made a harlot of my Bride

City of Righteousness

Faithful City

In ashes she wails and cries,

Hosea, Isaiah

You understand why?"

G od shone True

And spoke for the wise

"Nehemiah, Jeremiah

Look in to my eyes"

Jeremiah Wept

"God I am too young

And you made me Adept"

God in his command, Saith

Uproot. Overthrow. Tear down

Build and Plant

"Jeremiah what do you see?"

"Almond-shoot, I Am, Prophecy

The word of God came to me"

Shone Brightly. Spoke The Almighty

"Ezekiel come, towards me"

The Four Fold Way

Ezekiel did see

Left with the Ox

Right with the lion

Eagle and Man

Eyes on wheels

A rainbow around Zion

"Almighty"

Ezekiel fell to his knee

"El Shaddai, Adonai

We live in the dust

Of your feet

Above a dome

Adam came before me

I'd speak your words

Ezekiel spoke softly

There's no easy deal

Holy Ghost God of Host

I walk with thee"

And such he rose

To his feet

Sheppard after God's Heart

Heard he did

Herded God's Sheep

And to the Next Prophet

God did speak

"Moshae like Hosea

You'd know little sleep

My flock got stuck

Near waters' rough

And deep

Lead them to Green pastures

And Waters Still

To help them sleep

You'd lose None.

I've given Nun orders

That she will surely keep.

In the desert evil

Quench the thirsty

Take this staff and

Be shod in peace

Relieved the imprisoned

Believe Me creator of heaven

A murderer can give life in deed

Cain kills the abel'd

Not the Almond Seed".

Moshae picked up his staff

A DISCORD DANCE

The scent Roasted Almonds

Was on the breeze

"Almighty God I have to leave

The people need me"

God smiled bright

"You understand clearly".

T' was not for naught

David step forth

"Master what of me?

Little, I can do

Even something small

There must be?"

God shook his head

"David Play for me".

A harp he stroke, ten strings

God nodded and

Spoke great things

Indeed.

All great things you'll defeat

Thence. Samuel step forth

"Adonia your wisdom

Truly runs deep"

"Anoint Da-wood

Samuel"

God spoke softly

And turning to David

Samuel poured,

"Oh young Almond tree

In God's grace you'd

Grow to be mighty"

Daniel stood by David side

And God's radiance shone

Far and wide

"Daniel just rest a little while

For many of these seeds

Will be blown for miles

Driven under lashes

Sheep trampled when horses ride"

Daniel wept before the throne

Captivity of Joseph, the child

Captivity of Judah

"Oh Mount Sinai"

He walked, path of the lion

Dens full with pride

He did so for

The Holy Bride

Hosea spoke up

We must redeem

Every woman

Even Eve, Adam's Wife

Hosea took Gomer

God's' Words

"Go more than your pride

Scars shows' perfectly

What wrath hides".

God Spoke, as

Almighty The Wise

"Name him Jezreel

For the Massacre

The shedding of blood

Young lives,

Snuffed out

Before the High

She will be taken in captivity

These scars,

 Judah can't hide

My prophets may

Live to represent

The words of the wise

Walk the distance

Talk with insistence

Keep sacred remembrance

Be patient and penitent

Radiate my wisdom

You're heaven sent"

God Spoke to the Choir

Their elation rose higher

"The Almond seeds will repent

The stormy seas will relent

The prophecies

Their merriment

God's prophets

Born of men

God's promise

Save some of them

Who the cap fit

Will wear it then"

The Almighty words to them

"Many will waste away

Without a friend

I sent you to save

The widow, and

The orphaned

Released the prisoner

Break evil creations' like

Ibliss Coffin".

God smiled

"You get to witness

My works

For man

It's not often

You get

To see demon pigs fly

And demented snake coughing"

God smiled

"Did I mention?

Your powers unto

The last dimension?

Your ability to see the fiery arrows

The errors before the sorrows

You'll thrive where none can grow

Yacub, A foundation stone

    Jacob's rock a pillow"

God smiled

What do I know?

All his prophets', prophesized

The Almond Seeds grow

But in the end Ibliss

Dust devil blow

And one by one

Teeth, he showed

Sheep, he sheared

Birthed Grief for years

Humanity without

Their divinity,

Wrapped in robe.

Endlessly toiling

The earth in

Mud clung cloaks

Man fashioned

Mud slung works

Life in clay

Long they aged

Mingled with iron

Married their Irony

Shampooed their shame

Sooner than later God's

Prophecies Came

Home to roost

Roosters with a game

Ibliss rerouted

The roots regrouped

Some made lame

Others made lemonade

Ibliss slithered savage ways

Young prophets screamed out

For Brighter Days

God's Light shone

The Wailing and withered upon

Love, light, laughter, even

Bread none!

God Spoke "bun, everyone"

Love mingled with anger

God's showed mankind

Ibliss single fame

Darkened aim

Unclothed Ibliss shame

Wrath and Rage

God shone like Ishi.

The Flame

For Million of miles

No one smiled

God turned the Page.

"Young boy

Seed of Adam

What is your wage?

Young girl

Daughter of Eve

Of the world.

Why do you cry this way?"

God knew the answer

Born of free will

T was theirs to say

"Almighty we Gripes a lot

Grapes and nuts

When it falls off their plates"

God leaned forth

And wiped their tears away

Looking beyond them he

Saw the last days

"Oh little children

Did they not teach you to play?

Did they not reach you?

Like water to flowers in may.

Did they not keep you,

The way I did say?

Did they not care that your Angels

Are first before my ray?

Did they not give you beds'

Only dry leaves and hay?

Did they think Ancient of Days

Meant senile and grey?

Oh Little one's sit at my right side

This day"

God wept.

"I DIDN'T MAKE

Man This Way

I made him Kind

Kin King Kindred

Dead too many to say

Look how

They set about the young

Predators and prey

Angered prayers

They shout to clouds

Stir up dust I say

Ibliss lost and created

Souls Lust Full to sway

Family bust

Greed gluttony to fray

Envy and thieves

In a day

Gomer and Gomorrah

Brimstone Light this way

Firestone strikes in play".

Looking over his shoulder

God spoke that and this way

"The earth's my footstool

Am herald by an Angelic choir

Above me there's none higher

I made the heartless viper

I sent serpents Amen-Ra

I satisfy thirst and hunger

I made the last first

And old younger

Only in my name.

They can live longer

For gain,

They call oppressor master

Age means nothing for them

They undress the young faster

Slaves! All of them

They made objects their master

Prophecy will find them

Giving in marriage

Filled with lust and

Bitter laughter

The day of their destruction

Cometh swift and faster

Bishop hides shops

Of carnal pleasure?

I God seek and meet

Out measures.

They think their ways hidden

Ravings at leisure

Peeling young skins

For pleasures?

Hunting humans

A sporting feature?

I God created man,

Ibliss what's

Become

Of this creature?

Their gains they see

As a passing tes.t

But fallen man

Cannot be weightless".

"The goods they gain,

Slow down their trek

Happy is the fool

Who has only his step

For the rich, its only

At the end of life which corrects?

For the poor, only I God

Don't forget?

A cloven heel made

Mankind it's' pet?

I God gave you

Power over Ibliss

Many mansions

A kingdom of gifts

You traded it for an empty fist

Smoke filled mirrors

And illusions

You get the gist?

I God gave you, Eden

And you polluted all of it

Made you strong to

Help the weak

And it's them you've

Learn't to hit?!

What you did to the least of them

I repaying you all of it

Your cup overflow

With my wrath

I God pour more

Into it!

Drunkard of power

You should have learnt to sip!"

And all did see

Ibliss fell, he had no knee

Shaking an coiling fitfully

Annoyance, boiling restlessly

His features was plain

For all to see

Those who remain

Of him Shooked free

The naked king

The looks the glee

What did he think?

God spoil his works

For a flea?

A brash Nahash

That could not see?

A lunatic without a key?

A clue.

The mystery

Who knew

Ibliss was the last work

Of God To do

God Spoke quietly

"Everything but him

Existed perfectly"

He was the discord

God first heard amongst the choir

Refinement fine men God made

So Ibliss had to see

God's intention

Will mankind redemption, lead

Ibliss to accept,

God's' wisdom, as supreme?

Or is Ibliss the only creature,

God made purposefully mean?

God words came through clear

As day, no dream

"Ibliss need to be upright

For too long, his scales

Did unjustly lean".

God walked around the earth

"Its only destruction I've seen

Ibliss wasted his time

Hissing fumes and screams

There's nothing you can say

For yourself

Your words belong to me

There's no way you

Can create,

What my mind did foresee

You walk away

In rage

Led the world blindly

Took away the good king

Brute you made of the kindly"

Ibliss had no words

His breathe gone back to its herd

The breeze

Almightily

God was speaking

"Ibliss can't hear me

His senses are less

Because he spent freely

Without reserved

Coiling no coin in the king thief

No kindness to him

Who know not relief.

His essences

Was created by me

There's a lesson.

Here

Is how he'll learn mercy.

The method by which

I hung the universe

So perfectly"

And at Gods' right hand

The blue robe of Eve

Hung long

A song, sung

Lovingly

Glittering for a minute

Long enough

For Ibliss to see

And crying

His face screamed

"ee Eve, Even you can save me"

Eve face turned

Only Neith ninth night

Did Ibliss see,

Twelfth was in Sumer

And Ibliss under the sea.

Eve rose her magnificent

Magnified, by God's Grace and beauty

Slowly plucking Ibliss scales

She spoke softly

"Your radiance is hid

Under the muddy flecks

Of your deeds"

Each scale she peeled off

A thousand years, flew past

She hummed patiently

She had waited from the beginning

Before Cain made Able bleed

Each scale she plucked,

Ibliss let out a scream

Slowly the coils untangled

The unhinged un-seamed

Like a beautiful mirror

Foggy Under Steam

Struck dumb by Eves beauty

And caring mercy

Slowly did Ibliss

Vision gleaned

The woman he hurt

Ancient Eve

Was making him clean

Making him upright

Under scales of greed

That weight hung upon him

An made him a fallen seed

Fallen crest,

Deflated chest

Talents lost at a jest

Ibliss was beautiful

But mud marked as less.

For his words and his ways

Brought ruin to the best.

If only he could stand

An angel again,

Amongst the rest.

Or even a grain of sand

On God's regal dress

After centuries of hissing

Repressed

Ibliss struggled to smiled

While Eve

Untangled his

Mud mess.

Vines in his hair

And the plucks of his excess

Under the mud

Golden Rule, radiance,

One love

The choir erupted above

"God made Man from Mud

Mix it with wisdom and Love"

Eve evening sung

Ibliss radiance was redone

By Eve in the presence

Of every one.

It t'was a sight to see

Mud, flecks spurted off

Into the sea.

And Ibliss stood erect

Freed finally

From the curse

And by Mercy

Head higher

Not too high

Ibliss sung the whole

Night To Eve

Morning Star in the Sky

And to the Almighty

For the first time

Ibliss spoke kindly

"You surely made mud wise

I doubted, like the desert for water

Because my wells were dry

An seeing you busy making man

I tried, To make water

Instead I made the Prophets cry

Bitter water, not sweet waters

I dare not ask you

Because of pride,

I was created by your,

Everlasting love, and Desire.

And Eve's free will,

Cleansed my side"

Ibliss now spoke true

"If there's anything I can do"

And

God spoke as Almighty

The wise

"Stay longer than the rest

Until daylight, in the sky

Longer in my rays,

Will give you extra days

And you'd have to shine

Sing in my morning light.

Those who you've bitten

Will seek my face,

Shine long enough,

North Star to

Show them the way

To stand upright.

Ibliss stretched, his neck forth

Longer, no longer in fright

He'd lead the lost souls

Lust full foals

He'll be the first

To show Them, God's light

The beacon for the lost

And the way through,

The stormy night.

God's wisdom, mercy mingled

With his rays,

Great Love was his most

Profound might

The power of the will,

Will always be over flight.

Eve mercy,

Destruction stopped

God's Early

Ibliss struck sung

The last mud from his sight

And there he stands

Ill was his first deeds

Yet first in Morning's light

He once destroyed God's seeds

Now he forces them to see The Light

All Gods' Almond seeds

Planted in rows, tended in fields

Radiated Good deeds

The Vine forces them to be upright

God laughed,

His wisdom echoed

Through the cosmos

"With Mercy

I hung the universe

  Up Right".

Part Three

"Somewhere between History and Humility"

ABOUT THE PRODUCTION

THIS WORK OF POETRY was written for personal enjoyment and stage productions. Compiled from the literature traditions of Christianity, Judaism and Islam, this production may be beneficial to those interested in memorizing biblical details, or for learning simple nuances, of the various religious traditions. It incorporates humor and humility, with rhythmic verse and prose, illuminating and ensuring the reader will maintain the tempo as well as the images being conveyed in the poem. In Asè may you, Enjoy this rhythmic Journey of Early Biblical and Religious History.

ABOUT THE AUTHOR

A.M.K. ABERDEEN   mother, poet, painter, griot, scientists and historian, was born and raised in the Caribbean Diaspora. She began writing poetry at five years of age.

ABERDEEN, attended the University of Toronto, and study African and Caribbean history at University of the West Indies, Saint Augustine. She graduated with Bsc., in Forest Conservation, History and African Studies in 2011 from University of Toronto.

®Diadem Media LLC. © 2018

Notes

Notes

THIS PUBLICATION OF THE VINE COMEDY
A DISCORD DANCE

BELONGS' TO

www.ingramcontent.com/pod-product-compliance
Lightning Source LLC
Chambersburg PA
CBHW041614220426
43670CB00001B/17